HR Information Systems Integration Patterns

A guide to Architecture and Implementation

Sudheer Devaraju

Published by Ingram Content Group
ISBN: 979-8-3306-1330-4
First Edition: April 2021

Preface

In a world where technology drives every aspect of business, HR systems must continually adapt to meet the evolving needs of organizations and their workforces. As businesses grow and transform, the integration of disparate HR systems into a unified, effective platform becomes both a challenge and an opportunity. This book is my attempt to provide practical guidance to solution architects, HR technology leaders, and IT professionals who are tasked with designing and implementing these integrations.

Drawing on my years of experience in implementing HRIS solutions, particularly Workday, and lessons learned from a wide range of industries, this book captures the essence of what it takes to design integration architectures that are scalable, secure, and aligned with business goals. I aim to share insights gained from past implementations, highlighting industry-leading design patterns and proven strategies for overcoming the unique challenges of HRIS integration.

This guide is structured to equip solution architects and implementation teams with the tools and knowledge they need to succeed. Whether you're navigating the complexities of API-driven architectures, mastering hybrid integration patterns, or addressing compliance and security concerns, the frameworks and examples in these pages will provide actionable solutions and a roadmap for success.

Ultimately, this book is more than a technical manual—it's a reflection of the collaborative effort and problem-solving required to create HR systems that truly support an organization's people and processes. I hope it serves as both a practical resource and a source of inspiration as you tackle the challenges of HRIS integration and design solutions that make a lasting impact.

Let's build the future of HR systems together.

Acknowledgements

I want to express my heartfelt gratitude to my family and friends for their unwavering support during the creation of this book. A special thanks to my colleagues and mentors in the HRIS and IT community who inspired many of the ideas presented here.

Table of Contents

Introduction: Why Integration is Critical in HR Information Systems

HR Information Systems (HRIS) are foundational to any organization's workforce management strategy. These systems handle everything from recruitment and onboarding to payroll and benefits. However, when HR systems operate in isolation, data becomes fragmented, processes lack optimization, and alignment across the organization weakens. HRIS integration eliminates these gaps, enabling businesses to function seamlessly and make data-driven decisions with confidence.

1. Integration in HRIS

Integration in HRIS is not just a technical necessity—it's a strategic imperative. In today's fast-paced business environment, where agility and adaptability are vital, HRIS integration delivers several key benefits:

1.1 Unified Data for Better Decision-Making

When systems like Workday HCM, SAP SuccessFactors, and Oracle HR Cloud are integrated, data flows effortlessly across platforms. This integration simplifies processes, eliminates redundancies, reduces errors, and provides a single source of truth for HR and leadership teams. For instance, integrated payroll and benefits systems ensure that employee payslips are accurate and aligned with tax and compliance requirements.

1.2 Improved Employee Experience

Integration enhances the employee experience by facilitating seamless interaction with HR systems. For example, an employee portal with integrated back-end systems can provide access to leave balances, payslips, and training modules through a single dashboard, eliminating the need for multiple logins.

1.3 Operational Efficiency

Integration minimizes manual interventions, automates repetitive tasks, and reduces the risk of human error. For instance, SAP Payroll integrates with Workday's time tracking system, removing the need for manual data uploads and ensuring accurate payroll processing.

1.4 Regulatory Compliance

In highly regulated industries, integration ensures compliance-related data, such as employee tax details or labor law updates, is automatically and consistently applied across all HR systems. For example, Oracle HR Cloud can be integrated with local labor laws using built-in compliance features.

2. HRIS Integration Challenges

While integration offers significant benefits, it comes with its own set of challenges:

2.1 Legacy Systems

Many organizations still rely on outdated, on-premises systems that lack modern APIs. These systems make integration complex and costly.

2.2 Data Inconsistencies

Differences in data formats between systems can cause integration errors. For example, SAP SuccessFactors may use one naming convention for job titles, while Oracle HR Cloud uses another.

2.3 Security and Privacy

Integrated systems increase exposure to potential cyber threats. For instance, ensuring GDPR compliance in a multi-vendor HRIS ecosystem requires strong encryption and strict access controls.

Who Should Read This Book

This book is designed for a wide range of professionals involved in HRIS strategy, implementation, and management:

3.1 HR Technology Leaders

HR directors and managers seeking to enhance their processes and address common HRIS challenges will find this book invaluable. It provides actionable insights into integration patterns and solutions to common issues.

3.2 IT Architects and Developers

IT professionals responsible for designing and implementing integrations will gain technical knowledge of tools like Workday Studio, MuleSoft, and Apache Kafka.

3.3 Business Leaders

C-suite executives and decision-makers can learn about the strategic value of HRIS integration and how workforce strategies align with overall business objectives.

3.4 Consultants and System Implementers

Implementation experts working with platforms like Workday, SAP, and Oracle HR will find guidance on delivering scalable, future-proof solutions for their clients.

How This Book is Structured

This book is designed to take readers from foundational concepts to advanced integration techniques, offering both strategic and technical perspectives:

Chapter 1: HRIS Integration Fundamentals

This chapter introduces the value of integration, the components of an IIRIS, and the advantages of a unified system.

Chapter 2: HRIS Key Integration Patterns

Explore integration patterns like point-to-point, hub-and-spoke, and event-driven architecture. Each pattern is explained with real-world examples and use cases.

Chapter 3: Tools and Technologies of HRIS Integration

This chapter dives deep into tools like Workday Studio, APIs, and middleware platforms such as MuleSoft. Learn how to evaluate and select the right tools for your organization.

Chapter 4: Implementation Best Practices and Guide

This chapter offers practical advice on executing integration projects, ensuring data security, and achieving compliance. It includes case studies of successful integrations.

Conclusion

The book concludes with key takeaways and a discussion of HRIS integration trends, focusing on improving integration techniques, leveraging advanced reporting capabilities, and adapting to evolving business requirements.

Chapter 1: The Fundamentals of HRIS Integration

In today's fast-paced, data-driven business environment, organizations rely on a multitude of systems to manage their most valuable asset—their people. From applicant tracking and onboarding to payroll processing and performance management, HR Information Systems (HRIS) play a critical role in supporting the full employee lifecycle.

However, as HR technology stacks have grown more complex and specialized, so too has the challenge of ensuring that these systems work together seamlessly. Siloed data, disjointed processes, and inconsistent user experiences are all too common in organizations where HR systems are not properly integrated.

This is where HRIS integration comes in. By connecting and synchronizing key HR systems and data flows, organizations can unlock new efficiencies, insights, and experiences that would be impossible to achieve with standalone systems.

1.1 What is HRIS Integration?

HRIS integration refers to the seamless connection of the various digital frameworks that manage key workforce-related processes such as recruitment, payroll, time tracking, and benefits administration. The goal of integration is to enable data to flow freely between these systems, eliminating silos, reducing redundant data entry, and enabling real-time updates across platforms.

Integration ensures that different systems—often developed by different vendors such as Workday, SAP SuccessFactors, or Oracle HR—can communicate with one another effectively. For instance, integrating a time tracking system like Kronos or Workday Time Tracking with a payroll system ensures that employee hours are accurately reflected on payslips without the need for manual intervention.

Without integration, organizations face significant challenges such as:

- Fragmented and inconsistent employee data across systems
- Inefficiencies and delays in key HR processes like onboarding, payroll, and benefits enrollment
- Errors and compliance risks due to manual data handling and lack of real-time updates
- Inability to get a comprehensive, real-time view of the workforce for effective decision-making

In contrast, a well-integrated HRIS ecosystem empowers HR professionals to focus on strategic initiatives rather than troubleshooting disconnected systems. Integration enables:

- Streamlined and automated HR processes that improve efficiency and reduce errors
- Consistent and accurate employee data across all systems, enabling better workforce insights and decision-making
- Real-time updates and data synchronization across platforms, ensuring that all systems are working with the most current information
- Enhanced employee experience through self-service portals and seamless access to HR services and information

Integration is the backbone of an efficient and effective HRIS ecosystem. Without it, organizations struggle to fully leverage their HR technology investments and drive strategic business outcomes.

1.2 Key Components of HRIS

To understand the fundamentals of integration, it's essential to break down the major components of an HRIS. Each of these components serves a specific purpose but must work together seamlessly to deliver a cohesive HR experience.

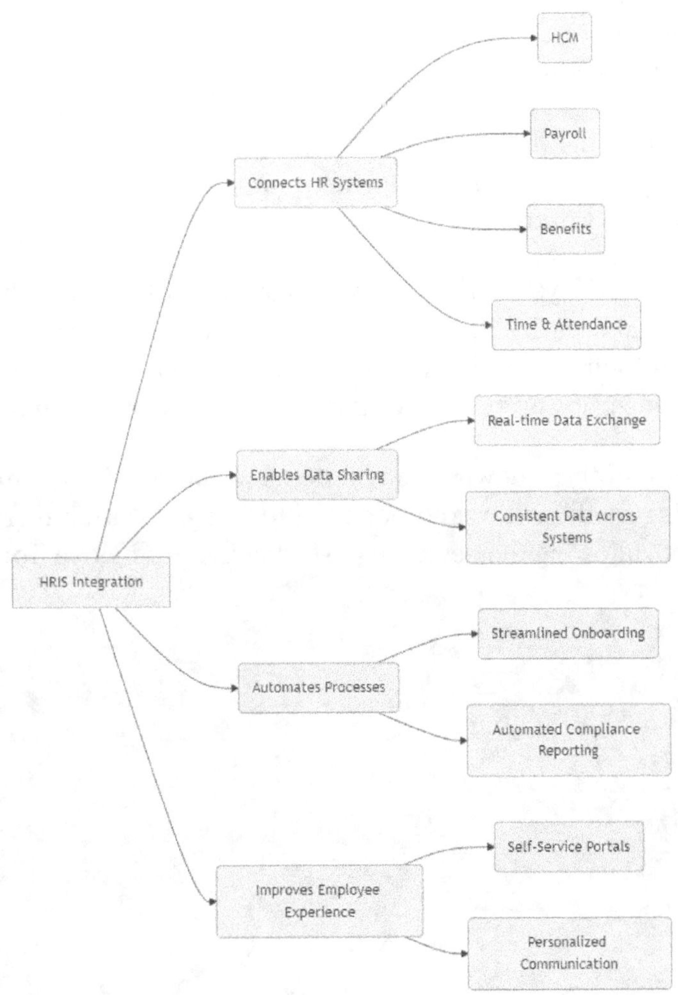

Fig: HRIS Integration Overview

1.2.1 Human Capital Management (HCM)

Human Capital Management (HCM) systems are at the core of any modern HRIS. These platforms, such as Workday HCM, SAP SuccessFactors Employee Central, and Oracle HCM Cloud, serve as the system of record for all employee data and manage key HR processes across the employee lifecycle.

Typical capabilities of an HCM system include:

- Employee data management (e.g., demographic information, job and compensation details, performance records)
- Organizational structure management (e.g., reporting hierarchies, position management)
- Talent acquisition and applicant tracking
- Onboarding and offboarding
- Performance management and goal setting
- Learning and development
- Succession planning and career development
- Compensation and rewards management
- HR analytics and reporting

HCM systems often serve as the "hub" for HR data and processes, with other HRIS components like payroll, time tracking, and benefits management integrating with the core HCM platform to exchange data and automate workflows.

For example, when a new employee is onboarded through Workday HCM, their core information (e.g., name, address, social security number, job title, salary) is automatically shared with the payroll system to set up their pay and tax withholdings, the benefits system to enroll them in eligible plans, and the time tracking system to start capturing their work hours.

Without integration, each of these downstream systems would require manual data entry to add the new hire, introducing inefficiencies and potential for errors. With integration, the process is seamless and automated, allowing the new hire to start being productive from day one.

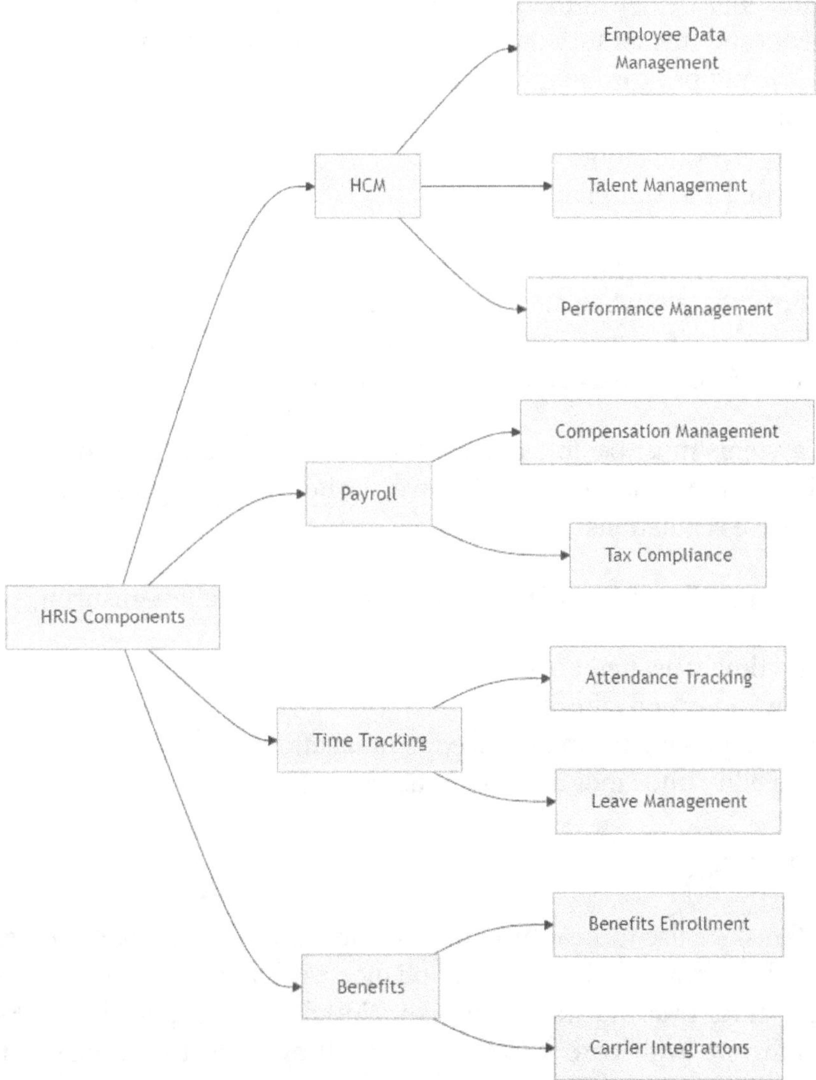

Fig: Key Components of HRIS

1.2.2 Payroll

Payroll systems are responsible for processing employee compensation, managing tax withholdings and deductions, and ensuring compliance with applicable labor laws and regulations. Leading payroll platforms like Workday Payroll, SAP SuccessFactors Employee Central Payroll, and Oracle Payroll integrate closely with core HCM systems to exchange employee and pay data.

Key capabilities of payroll systems include:

- Employee pay calculation and processing (e.g., salary, hourly wages, bonuses, commissions)
- Tax withholdings and filings (e.g., federal, state, and local taxes)

- Benefit deductions (e.g., health insurance premiums, retirement plan contributions)
- Garnishments and involuntary deductions (e.g., child support, tax levies)
- Direct deposit and pay card management
- Payroll accounting and general ledger integration
- Labor allocation and costing
- Payroll reporting and compliance

Payroll systems rely heavily on data from other HRIS components, particularly HCM and time tracking systems. For example, when an employee receives a promotion and pay raise in the HCM system, that updated salary information must be seamlessly passed to the payroll system to ensure the employee's next paycheck reflects their new rate of pay.

Similarly, payroll systems must be able to consume work hours and attendance data from time tracking systems in order to accurately calculate pay for hourly employees and ensure compliance with overtime and leave regulations.

Integration between payroll and other HRIS components is critical for ensuring:

- Accurate and timely payment of employees
- Compliance with tax and labor laws
- Efficient payroll processing and reduced manual effort
- Real-time visibility into labor costs and budgets

1.2.3 Time Tracking

Time tracking systems are used to capture and manage employee work hours, schedule shifts, track attendance and absences, and ensure compliance with labor regulations like overtime and leave laws. Leading time tracking platforms like Workday Time Tracking, Kronos, and ADP Workforce Now integrate with core HCM and payroll systems to automate data flows and processes.

Key capabilities of time tracking systems include:

- Employee time capture (e.g., clock-in/clock-out, timesheet entry)
- Absence and leave management (e.g., paid time off requests and approvals, leave balance tracking)
- Scheduling and shift management
- Overtime calculation and compliance
- Mobile and web-based interfaces for employee self-service
- Real-time labor analytics and reporting

Time tracking data is critical for payroll processing, labor cost management, and workforce planning. Integrating time tracking systems with payroll ensures that employees are paid accurately based on their actual hours worked, including any overtime or premium pay.

Integration with HCM systems allows time off requests and approvals to flow seamlessly into employee records and downstream processes like scheduling and payroll. For example, when an employee requests a vacation day through the time tracking system, that request can automatically be routed to their manager for approval based on configured business rules and workflows. Once approved, the employee's time off balance is decremented in the HCM system, and the absence is reflected in the payroll system for accurate pay calculation.

Real-world example: Acme Corporation uses Workday HCM and Workday Time Tracking. When an hourly employee works overtime, their extra hours are automatically captured in Workday Time Tracking and synced to Workday Payroll for inclusion in their next paycheck. This integration saves Acme's payroll team hours of manual data entry each pay period and ensures employees are paid correctly for their time worked.

1.2.4 Benefits Administration

Benefits administration systems manage employee health and welfare benefits, including medical, dental, and vision insurance, life and disability insurance, flexible spending accounts, health savings accounts, and retirement plans. These systems integrate with HCM and payroll systems to streamline benefits enrollment, changes, and deductions.

Key capabilities of benefits administration systems include:

- Online benefits enrollment and life event management
- Eligibility rules management and enforcement
- Provider and plan management
- Premium and deduction calculations
- Carrier connectivity and data exchange
- ACA compliance and reporting

Integrating benefits systems with HCM platforms enables employee demographic and job information to flow automatically into the benefits system, ensuring that employees are enrolled in the correct plans based on their eligibility and that deductions are accurately calculated and passed to payroll.

For example, when a new hire completes their onboarding tasks in the HCM system, they can seamlessly access the benefits enrollment process and select their coverage options. Their elections are captured in the benefits system and automatically trigger the appropriate payroll deductions without any manual intervention.

Real-world example: Global Enterprises uses SAP SuccessFactors Employee Central and SAP SuccessFactors Benefits. During open enrollment, employees log into the SAP SuccessFactors portal to review and update their benefit elections for the upcoming year. These elections are automatically synced to SAP Payroll to start the appropriate deductions on the first paycheck of the new plan year. This integration allows Global Enterprises to process open enrollment for thousands of employees with minimal manual effort and fewer errors.

1.3 Common Challenges in HR System Integration

While the benefits of HRIS integration are significant, successfully connecting and synchronizing HR systems comes with a unique set of challenges that organizations must overcome.

1.3.1 Legacy Systems

Many organizations still rely on outdated, on-premise HR systems that were never designed with integration in mind. These legacy platforms often lack modern APIs and integration capabilities, making it difficult and costly to connect them with newer cloud-based systems.

For example, an organization using a 20-year-old, custom-built payroll system may struggle to integrate it with a modern SaaS HCM platform like Workday or SAP SuccessFactors. The legacy system may store data in proprietary formats, have limited integration points, or require significant custom development to enable data exchange.

To overcome this challenge, organizations may need to invest in middleware solutions or custom-built integrations to bridge the gap between old and new systems. In some cases, the best path forward may be to replace legacy systems entirely with modern, integration-friendly platforms.

1.3.2 Data Consistency and Quality

Another common challenge in HRIS integration is ensuring data consistency and quality across disparate systems. Different HR platforms often have their own data models, field definitions, and naming conventions, which can lead to integration errors and data discrepancies.

For example, an HCM system may track employee job titles using a free-text field, while the payroll system uses a fixed set of job codes. Integrating these systems requires mapping and transforming data between the two formats, which can be complex and error-prone.

Additionally, data quality issues in one system can quickly propagate to other integrated systems, leading to a domino effect of errors and inconsistencies. For instance, if an employee's name is misspelled in the HCM system, that incorrect data will flow through to payroll, benefits, and other downstream systems.

To mitigate these challenges, organizations need to establish strong data governance practices and implement robust data quality controls as part of their integration strategy. This may include:

- Defining standard data models and field mappings across systems
- Implementing data validation and cleansing routines to catch and fix errors
- Establishing data stewardship roles and processes to ensure ongoing data quality
- Investing in data integration and quality tools to automate and monitor data flows

1.3.3 Security and Compliance

Integrating HR systems also introduces new security and compliance risks. As sensitive employee data flows between multiple systems and potentially outside the organization (e.g., to benefit carriers or payroll providers), it becomes more vulnerable to unauthorized access, breaches, or misuse.

Organizations must ensure that their HRIS integration architecture is designed with security and compliance in mind. This includes:

- Implementing strong access controls and authentication mechanisms to ensure only authorized users can access and modify HR data
- Encrypting sensitive data both at rest and in transit to protect against interception or theft
- Regularly monitoring system logs and audit trails to detect and respond to security events
- Conducting thorough security assessments and penetration tests to identify and remediate vulnerabilities
- Ensuring compliance with relevant data privacy and security regulations, such as GDPR, HIPAA, or SOC 2

Real-world example: A healthcare provider implementing an integrated HRIS must ensure that all data flows and integrations comply with HIPAA regulations for protecting patient information. This includes encrypting data in transit, implementing strict access controls, and maintaining detailed audit trails of all system interactions. The provider must also have Business Associate Agreements (BAAs) in place with any third-party integration partners that handle protected health information.

1.4 Benefits of a Well-Integrated HRIS

When done right, HRIS integration can drive significant business value and operational benefits. A well-integrated HR technology ecosystem can help organizations to:

1.4.1 Streamline HR Processes

Integration automates manual data entry and routing tasks, reducing the time and effort required to complete common HR processes like onboarding, transfers, and terminations. With integrated systems, data flows seamlessly across platforms without the need for human intervention, allowing HR teams to focus on more strategic work.

For example, a well-integrated HRIS can automatically route new hire data from the applicant tracking system to the HCM system for onboarding, then to the payroll and benefits systems for enrollment and processing. This eliminates the need for HR staff to manually re-enter data at each step, saving time and reducing errors.

1.4.2 Enhance Employee Experience

Integration also enables organizations to deliver a more seamless and consumer-like experience to employees. With an integrated HRIS, employees can access all their HR information and services through a single, unified portal rather than logging into multiple disparate systems.

For example, an employee might use a single sign-on to access their pay stubs, benefits enrollment, time off requests, and performance reviews all from one centralized hub. This saves time and frustration for employees and makes it easier for them to find the information they need.

Real-world example: NetSuite Corporation uses Oracle HCM Cloud and Oracle Employee Self-Service to provide a unified portal for all employee HR needs. Employees can log in to view their pay slips, enroll in benefits, request time off, and update their personal information all in one place. This integrated approach has significantly increased employee satisfaction and reduced HR support requests.

1.4.3 Improve Data-Driven Decision Making

By integrating HR data across systems, organizations gain a more complete and accurate picture of their workforce. With real-time access to comprehensive people data, HR leaders and business managers can make more informed decisions about talent strategies, workforce planning, and operational improvements.

For example, integrating HCM data with learning management and performance systems might reveal that employees who complete certain training programs have higher rates of promotions and retention. Armed with this insight, HR could double down on those programs as part of their talent development strategy.

Real-world example: Coca-Cola uses SAP SuccessFactors and SAP Analytics Cloud to integrate HR data across the enterprise and deliver actionable workforce insights. By combining data from core HR, talent management, and learning systems, Coca-Cola can identify skills gaps, predict future hiring needs, and measure the business impact of HR programs. This integrated approach to people analytics has helped Coca-Cola to optimize its talent strategies and drive better business outcomes.

1.4.4 Reduce Compliance Risks

Integrated HR systems also help organizations to manage compliance with increasingly complex labor and tax regulations. By automating key compliance workflows and ensuring consistent data across systems, organizations can reduce the risk of errors, audits, and penalties.

For example, an integrated payroll and time tracking system can automatically apply the correct overtime rates and pay rules based on an employee's location and job classification, ensuring compliance with federal and state wage and hour laws. Similarly, an integrated benefits system can help employers to comply with ACA reporting requirements by automatically tracking employee eligibility and coverage data and generating the necessary forms and filings.

Real-world example: XYZ Inc. uses ADP SmartCompliance and ADP Workforce Now to manage HR compliance across its 50-state operations. By integrating payroll, time and attendance, and HR data, ADP SmartCompliance automates key compliance tasks like new hire reporting, wage garnishments, and unemployment claims management. This integrated approach has saved XYZ Inc. countless hours of manual compliance work and reduced their risk of costly penalties and litigation.

1.4.5 Enable Agile HR Service Delivery

Integration enables HR organizations to be more agile and responsive to changing business needs. With seamless data flows and automated processes, HR can quickly adapt to organizational changes like restructurings, mergers and acquisitions, and global expansions.

For example, if a company acquires a new subsidiary, an integrated HRIS can quickly onboard the new employees and ensure they are set up correctly in all relevant systems (HCM, payroll, benefits, etc.). This allows the newly acquired employees to hit the ground running and reduces the administrative burden on HR.

1.4.6 Drive Continuous Improvement

Finally, a well-integrated HRIS provides the foundation for continuous improvement of HR processes and technology. With integrated systems and data, organizations can more easily identify inefficiencies, bottlenecks, and areas for optimization.

Chapter 2: Key Integration Patterns in HRIS

In the last chapter, we took a deep dive into the world of HRIS integration, exploring why it's so crucial for modern HR service delivery. We looked at the key pieces of the HRIS puzzle, the benefits of getting integration right, and the common pitfalls that organizations face when connecting their HR systems.

Now, it's time to roll up our sleeves and get into the nitty-gritty of how integration actually works. In this chapter, we'll explore three of the most common integration patterns used in HR environments: point-to-point, hub-and-spoke, and event-driven architectures. We'll break down the pros and cons of each approach and look at some real-world examples of how they're used to connect HR systems like Workday, SAP SuccessFactors, and Oracle.

By the end of this chapter, you'll have a solid grasp of the different integration strategies available and when to use them based on your unique HR needs and tech constraints. So, grab a cup of coffee, get comfy, and let's dive in!

2.1 Point-to-Point Integration

If you're just getting started with HR integration, point-to-point (P2P) is probably the first approach that comes to mind. It's simple, it's straightforward, and it's been around for ages. In a nutshell, P2P integration involves creating direct, one-to-one connections between your HR systems, allowing them to share data without any middleman.

Think of it like a game of telephone, but without the risk of garbled messages. System A talks directly to System B, passing along employee data, payroll info, benefits elections, you name it. System B might then turn around and pass some of that data along to System C, and so on.

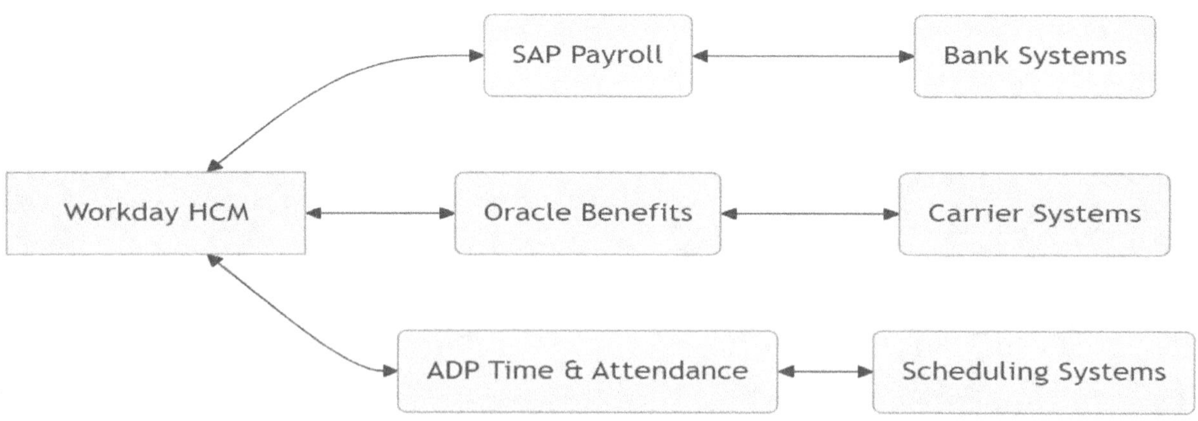

Fig: Point to Point Integration

2.1.1 When to Use Point-to-Point Integration

So, when does it make sense to use P2P integration? Well, if you've got a small HR tech stack with just a handful of systems, P2P can be a great choice. It's relatively easy to set up and maintain those direct connections when you're only dealing with a few moving parts.

P2P is also a good option if you need to get an integration up and running quickly. Because it's so straightforward, you can often get a P2P integration in place faster than some of the more complex approaches we'll discuss later.

And let's not forget about cost. If you're working with a tight budget, P2P can be a more affordable way to get your HR systems talking to each other, since you don't need to invest in any fancy middleware or integration platforms.

But, there's a catch. While P2P works great for small, simple HR environments, it can quickly turn into a nightmare as you add more systems to the mix. Imagine trying to maintain separate connections between a dozen different HR platforms - it's like untangling a massive ball of spaghetti!

Every time you add a new system, you've got to build out a whole new set of integrations. And if something changes in one of those systems (like a software update or a new data field), you've got to update all of those connections individually. It's a maintenance headache waiting to happen.

2.1.2 Practical Examples in HRIS

Despite its limitations, P2P integration is still really common in HR environments, especially for simple, one-way data sharing between core systems.

For example, let's say you're using Workday as your main HCM platform and SAP Payroll for paying your people. You might set up a P2P integration to automatically send employee data (like salaries, hours worked, and tax info) from Workday to SAP Payroll each pay period. That way, your payroll team doesn't have to manually key in all that data every two weeks.

Or maybe you're using Oracle for your core HR needs and a standalone benefits platform to manage things like health insurance and 401(k) enrollments. A P2P integration could make sure that any time an employee makes a change to their benefits in Oracle (like adding a new baby to their health plan), that change automatically flows over to your benefits system too. No more annoying data discrepancies or missed deductions.

The key with P2P is to use it judiciously. It's great for those simple, high-volume data flows between a small number of systems. But as soon as you start adding more complexity, like multi-step workflows or data transformations, it's time to look at a more robust approach.

2.2 Hub-and-Spoke Integration

If point-to-point is the trusty old bicycle of HR integration, hub-and-spoke (H&S) is the sleek, modern sports car. H&S tackles the scalability issues of P2P by introducing a central "hub" (typically a middleware platform or an Enterprise Service Bus) that sits in the middle of your HR systems and handles all the data traffic.

Instead of each system having to maintain separate connections to every other system, they only need to connect to the hub. The hub takes care of the rest, routing data to the right places, translating it into the right formats, and orchestrating more complex workflows.

Picture a wheel with the hub at the center and each of your HR systems as the spokes. Data flows into the hub from one system, gets processed and transformed as needed, and then gets sent back out to one or more other systems. It's a much more efficient way to manage data flow, especially as you scale up.

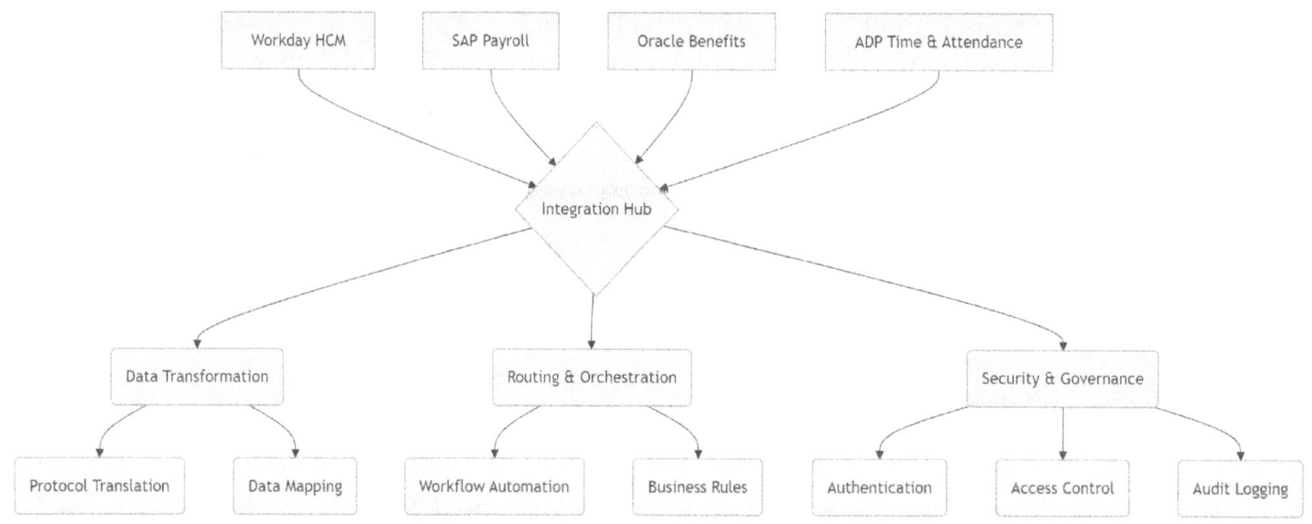

Fig: Hub-and-Spoke Integration

2.2.1 Overview of Middleware and ESBs

So what exactly is this "hub," and how does it work? In most cases, it's implemented using a middleware platform or an Enterprise Service Bus (ESB). These tools act as a central switchboard for your HR integration, providing a bunch of key capabilities:

- **Protocol Translation:** Your HR systems might "speak" different languages in terms of how they send and receive data (like XML, JSON, or CSV files). Middleware can translate between these different protocols, so your systems can communicate smoothly.
- **Data Transformation:** Often, the data coming out of one HR system isn't in quite the right format for another system. Maybe the field names are different, or the data needs to be split up or combined in a certain way. Middleware can handle these data transformations on the fly, so each system gets the data in the format it expects.

- **Routing and Orchestration:** In more complex integrations, data might need to flow through multiple steps or be routed based on certain conditions. For example, a new hire workflow might need to first create the employee record in your HCM system, then trigger onboarding tasks in your learning platform, and finally send a notification to your IT team to provision system access. Middleware can orchestrate these multi-step workflows and make sure data gets routed to the right places based on predefined rules.
- **Security and Governance:** Because middleware acts as a central hub for HR data, it's also a great place to enforce security, access controls, and compliance rules. You can set up authentication and authorization at the hub level, so only the right systems and users can access sensitive HR data. And you can centrally monitor and log all data flows for auditing and troubleshooting.

Some of the most popular middleware and ESB tools for HR integration include MuleSoft, Dell Boomi, IBM App Connect, and Oracle Integration Cloud. These platforms provide pre-built connectors for common HR systems, drag-and-drop integration builders, and lots of other handy features to make integration easier.

2.2.2 Use Cases in HR Environments

H&S integration is a great fit for HR departments that are dealing with a lot of different systems and complex data flows. Here are a few common scenarios where it really shines:

Employee Onboarding and Offboarding: Getting a new employee set up (or shutting down access when someone leaves) involves a ton of different HR systems - HCM, payroll, benefits, learning, IT provisioning, and so on. With H&S, you can orchestrate all of those different steps through your central hub. So when a new hire record is created in your HCM system, it can automatically trigger provisioning requests in your IT systems, benefits enrollments, and training assignments, all without manual effort.

Cross-System Workflows: A lot of HR processes touch multiple systems, like performance reviews that involve data from your HCM, talent, and compensation planning platforms. With H&S, you can automate these end-to-end workflows through the hub. So when a manager submits a performance review in your talent system, it can automatically update the employee record in your HCM system, calculate any compensation changes, and even kick off a career development discussion in your learning platform.

HR Analytics and Reporting: To get a true picture of your workforce, you often need to pull data from a bunch of different HR systems - headcount and demographic data from your HCM platform, engagement scores from your survey tool, learning completions from your LMS, and so on. Middleware can act as a central data integration layer, pulling all of that HR data into a single data warehouse or reporting platform, so you've got one trusted source of people analytics.

2.3 Event-Driven Integration

So far, we've looked at integration approaches that are all about moving data between systems on a regular schedule - whether that's a nightly batch feed or a real-time sync triggered by a specific workflow. But what if you need your HR systems to be able to share data instantly, the moment something changes?

That's where event-driven integration comes in. In this approach, your HR systems can publish "events" whenever something important happens - like an employee getting promoted, a new hire completing onboarding, or a manager submitting a time-off request. Other systems can then subscribe to those events and take immediate action, without waiting for a scheduled data sync.

It's kind of like social media notifications. When someone tags you in a post or comments on your photo, you get pinged right away. You don't have to keep refreshing your feed to see what's new - the important stuff comes to you. Event-driven integration applies that same principle to your HR data.

2.3.1 Real-Time Data Exchange

The beauty of event-driven integration is that it enables true real-time data flow between your HR systems. The moment an event occurs in one system, that data can be instantly pushed out to all the other systems that need it. No more lag times or stale data.

This real-time exchange is especially important for certain HR scenarios, like:

- **Compliance and Security:** When an employee is terminated, you need to immediately cut off their access to all your HR systems. If you're relying on a nightly batch feed to update your IT provisioning platform, that terminated employee could still have access for hours or even days. With event-driven integration, the moment the termination is recorded in your HCM system, an event can be triggered to instantly deprovision their accounts across all systems.
- **Payroll Accuracy:** Payroll errors are costly and frustrating for everyone involved. Event-driven integration can help ensure your payroll is always accurate by instantly pushing any pay-impacting changes (like a raise or a bonus) from your HCM system to your payroll platform. No more worrying about missing a pay change because it didn't get synced in time for the next payroll run.
- **Benefits Administration:** Likewise, event-driven integration is a lifesaver for benefits administrators. When an employee has a qualifying life event (like getting married or having a baby), they need their benefits updated ASAP. With real-time event triggers, the moment that life event is recorded in your benefits platform, it can automatically update the employee record in your HCM and payroll systems too. No manual data entry required.

2.3.2 Practical Use Cases

Alright, enough theory - let's look at some real-world examples of event-driven integration in action for HR:

Instant Employee Record Updates: Let's say you're using Workday for core HR and a separate system for IT provisioning. Whenever an employee's job title, location, or manager changes in Workday, you need that update reflected immediately in your IT system so their access and permissions stay current.

With event-driven integration, you can set up Workday to publish an "Employee Updated" event any time one of those key fields is changed. Your IT system can subscribe to that event and instantly update the employee record on their end, triggering any necessary access changes. No more worrying about employees having the wrong permissions because of outdated data.

Real-Time Performance Management: Or maybe you use SAP SuccessFactors for performance management and a homegrown HR data warehouse for people analytics. Every time a performance review is completed in SuccessFactors, you want that data available right away in your warehouse so your analytics are always up to date.

By setting up event-based integration, SuccessFactors can publish a "Review Completed" event whenever a review is finalized, including the overall rating and any key metrics. Your data warehouse can listen for that event and instantly incorporate the new review data into your performance dashboards and reports. No more waiting for a batch process to run overnight.

Summary

And there you have it - a whirlwind tour of the three most common integration patterns in the world of HR tech! We've covered a lot of ground, so let's recap the key points:

1. **Point-to-Point (P2P) Integration:** The simplest approach, P2P involves direct connections between individual HR systems. It's great for small environments and straightforward data sharing, but can quickly get messy as you add more systems.
2. **Hub-and-Spoke (H&S) Integration:** H&S introduces a central middleware layer that acts as a hub for all your integration needs - data transformation, routing, orchestration, and more. It's ideal for larger HR tech stacks and more complex workflows.
3. **Event-Driven Integration:** This approach enables real-time data sharing by having systems publish and subscribe to data "events." It's perfect for scenarios where you need instant updates, like compliance, payroll, and benefits administration.

Of course, these patterns aren't one-size-fits-all. The right approach for your organization will depend on a bunch of factors - the size and complexity of your HR systems landscape, the types of data you need to share, your budget and resources, and more.

Many organizations use a mix of patterns, like H&S for the core HR systems and event-driven for specific real-time needs. The key is to have a clear integration strategy that aligns with your overall HR tech roadmap.

Now that we've got the lay of the integration land, our next stop on this journey is diving into the nitty-gritty of how to actually implement these patterns using the latest and greatest HR integration tools and platforms. We'll look at some of the most popular middleware options, walk through some hands-on examples, and share best practices from real-world HR integration projects.

Chapter 3: Tools and Technologies Designed for HRIS Integration

Welcome back, dear reader! In previous chapters, we explored HRIS integration patterns, diving into the benefits and challenges of point-to-point, hub-and-spoke, and event-driven architectures. We also discussed when to use them in real-world HR scenarios. However, seasoned integration architects will agree that choosing the right pattern is only half the battle. To complete your integration vision, you need the right tools and technologies.

In this chapter, we will delve into some of the most popular and powerful integration tools available, such as Workday Studio, MuleSoft, and Apache Kafka. Additionally, we will examine the roles of APIs and webhooks in modern HRIS integration and explore how data transformation tools like XSLT and Informatica help tackle complex data formats. Recognizing that technology choices do not exist in isolation, we'll also discuss cloud vs. on-premise integration models and how to choose the best deployment scheme for your business.

Whether you're a seasoned integration guru or just beginning your HRIS journey, this chapter will equip you with the knowledge and tools to tackle even the most challenging integrations. Let's dive in!

3.1 Overview of Common Tools

The HR technology landscape offers a wide array of tools and platforms for HRIS integration. In this section, we will focus on three of the most popular tools: Workday Studio, MuleSoft, and Apache Kafka.

3.1.1 Workday Studio

If Workday is your core HCM platform, chances are you've already encountered Workday Studio. Integrated seamlessly into the Workday environment, it allows you to build, test, and deploy integrations without leaving the Workday ecosystem.

Workday Studio was specifically designed with HR integration use cases in mind and includes connectors to common HR systems like SAP SuccessFactors, Oracle HCM, and ADP. Its drag-and-drop interface empowers even non-technical users to create simple integrations without writing code.

However, don't let its user-friendly interface fool you—Workday Studio is a robust enterprise-grade integration tool. It supports various integration patterns, from simple data synchronization to complex event-driven workflows. With features like error handling, data transformation, and real-time monitoring, Workday Studio ensures that your integrations are reliable and scalable.

Example Use Case:

- Create a new integration in Workday Studio by selecting SAP SuccessFactors as the connector.
- Use the visual mapping tool to align data fields between Workday and SuccessFactors.
- Define data synchronization timing and error-handling logic.
- Test the integration using Workday Studio's built-in tools.
- Deploy the integration to production with just a few clicks.

3.1.2 MuleSoft

For organizations looking for a general-purpose integration platform, MuleSoft offers unparalleled versatility. Its Anypoint Platform provides a unified environment for API design, implementation, and management. Whether your systems are on-premise or in the cloud, MuleSoft allows you to connect applications, data sources, and devices seamlessly.

MuleSoft's extensive library of connectors and templates includes HR-specific integrations for tools like Workday, SAP SuccessFactors, and Oracle HCM. With prebuilt templates for common HR tasks such as employee onboarding and benefits enrollment, you can accelerate integration timelines and minimize complexity.

MuleSoft is not just about speed—it's highly scalable and robust. Features like auto-scaling, high availability, and real-time monitoring make it an excellent choice for demanding integration workloads.

Example Use Case:

- Create a new Mule project in Anypoint Studio and add connectors for Workday and Salesforce.
- Define data sources and endpoints using APIs like the Workday Employee API and Salesforce User Object.
- Use Anypoint DataWeave to map and transform data.
- Configure error handling and test the integration locally using MuleSoft's built-in tools.
- Deploy the integration to the Anypoint Platform for runtime management and monitoring.

3.1.3 Apache Kafka

While most integration tools focus on moving data between systems, Apache Kafka specializes in processing massive streams of real-time data. As an open-source stream-processing framework, Kafka enables systems to publish and consume data streams without worrying about the source or destination of the data.

In an HR context, Kafka excels in event-driven architectures. For example, if an employee's job title or department changes in an HCM system, Kafka publishes this change to a topic. Downstream systems like payroll or organizational chart tools can subscribe to this topic and react in real time.

Kafka's ability to scale horizontally across multiple nodes or data centers makes it incredibly resilient. Its data replication and persistence features ensure that no data is lost, even in the event of node failure.

Example Use Case:

- Configure an integration in Workday Studio to publish employee data changes to a Kafka topic.
- Downstream systems subscribe to the Kafka topic to receive real-time updates on employee changes.
- Use stream-processing frameworks like Kafka Streams to enrich and transform the data.
- Save enriched data to a data warehouse for reporting and analytics.

3.2 HRIS Integration with APIs and Webhooks

APIs and webhooks are fundamental to modern HRIS integration. APIs (Application Programming Interfaces) define how two systems communicate, specifying the requests a system can accept, the expected data formats, and the responses it will return. Webhooks, on the other hand, enable real-time communication by "pushing" data from one system to another when specific events occur.

APIs in HRIS

APIs are widely used in HR systems to expose data and functionality to other platforms. For example, an HCM system might have an API to provide employee compensation data, while a payroll system might expose APIs to retrieve this data for reporting purposes. APIs allow systems to communicate regardless of their underlying technologies, as long as they adhere to the same protocol (e.g., REST or SOAP).

Webhooks in HRIS

Webhooks enable event-driven integrations by notifying other systems when specific events occur. For instance, a candidate tracking system can use a webhook to notify an HCM system when a candidate is hired. The HCM system can then automatically create a new employee record and initiate the onboarding process.

By combining APIs and webhooks, organizations can build flexible, responsive systems that support real-time data sharing and automation. This modern approach to integration enables HR teams to adapt quickly to changing business needs.

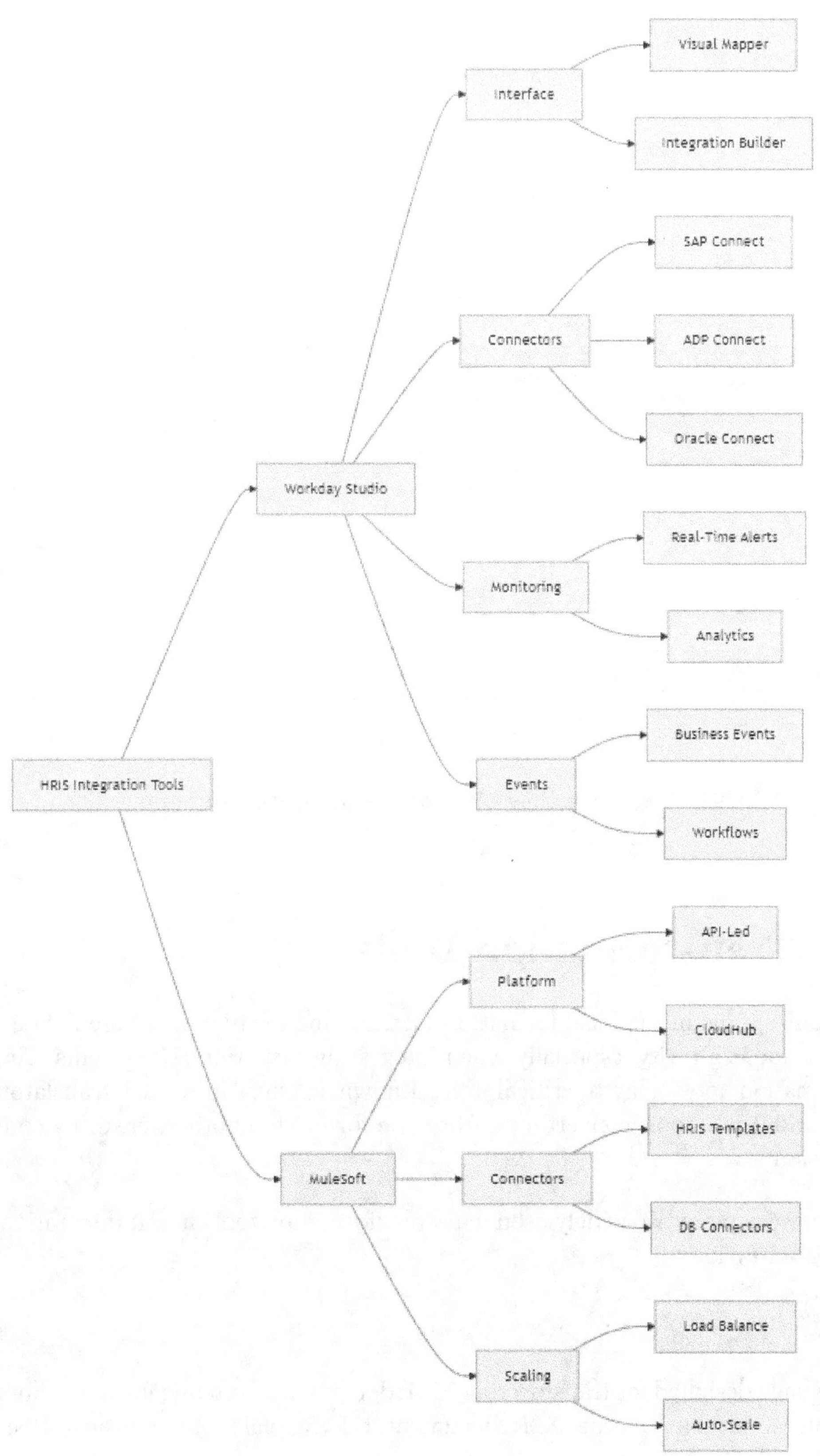

HRIS Integration Tools
Workday Studio
Interface
Visual Mapper
Integration Builder
Connectors
SAP Connect
ADP Connect
Oracle Connect
Monitoring
Real-Time Alerts
Analytics
Events
Business Events
Workflows
MuleSoft
Platform
API-Led
CloudHub
Connectors
HRIS Templates
DB Connectors
Scaling
Load Balance
Auto-Scale

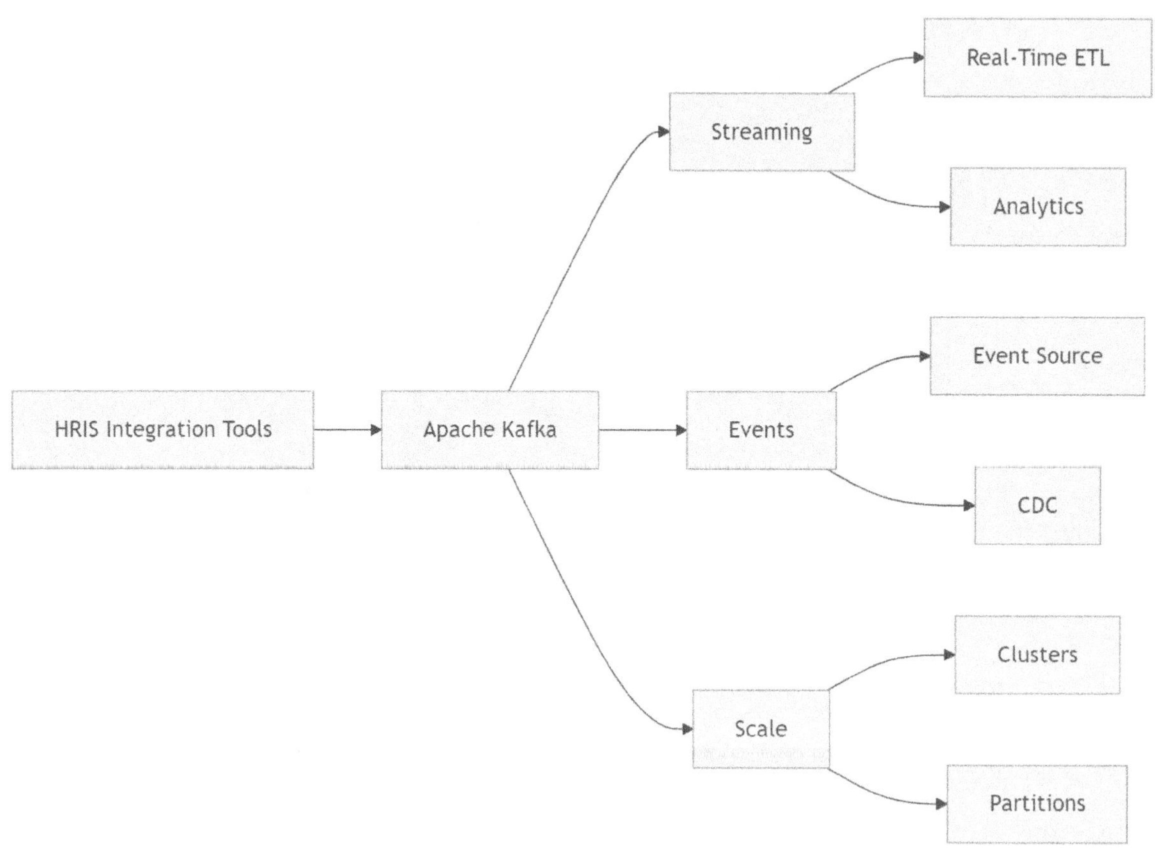

Fig: HRIS Tools Overview - Workday Studio, MuleSoft and Kafka

3.3 Data Transformation Tools

Data rarely comes to us in the ideal format. In fact, finding a situation where data arrives in a ready-to-use shape is a rarity, especially when integrating disparate HR systems. That's where data transformation tools play a critical role. Known as the "universal translators" of the integration world, these tools convert data from one format to another, ensuring compatibility with target systems.

In this section, we explore two widely used data transformation tools in HR integration projects: **XSLT** and **Informatica**.

3.3.1 XSLT

XSLT is a language designed for transforming XML documents from one format to another. The transformation can produce another XML document, HTML, plain text, or even JSON.

In HR integration, XSLT plays a vital role in bridging the gap between systems by transforming employee data as it moves between them. For instance, when integrating Workday HCM with

ADP Payroll, XSLT helps convert Workday's exported XML format into the structure required by ADP.

Example Transformation:
In this example, we transform a Workday_Employee XML format into an ADP_Employee XML structure:

xml

Copy code

```xml
<xsl:stylesheet xmlns:xsl="http://www.w3.org/1999/XSL/Transform" version="1.0">
  <xsl:template match="/">
   <ADP_Employee>
    <EmployeeID>
     <xsl:value-of select="Workday_Employee/Employee_ID"/>
    </EmployeeID>
    <FirstName>
     <xsl:value-of select="Workday_Employee/First_Name"/>
    </FirstName>
    <LastName>
     <xsl:value-of select="Workday_Employee/Last_Name"/>
    </LastName>
    <Title>
     <xsl:value-of select="Workday_Employee/Job_Title"/>
    </Title>
   </ADP_Employee>
  </xsl:template>
</xsl:stylesheet>
```

In this transformation, fields like Employee_ID, First_Name, Last_Name, and Job_Title from Workday's format are mapped to corresponding fields in ADP's format.

XSLT supports advanced features like conditionals, loops, and function calls, making it powerful for complex transformations. It is widely supported by integration platforms and ESBs, making it a go-to tool for straightforward transformations. However, its complexity can become a challenge for maintaining mappings as datasets grow or involve intricate logic.

3.3.2 Informatica

Informatica is a comprehensive platform designed to handle data transformation, quality, governance, and more. It is widely used for large-scale HR migrations, master data management, and ongoing synchronization between core HR systems like Workday, SAP SuccessFactors, and Oracle HCM.

A standout feature of Informatica is its **Mapping Designer**, a visual interface that allows users to define data transformations without writing code. With its drag-and-drop interface, business analysts and data stewards can manage data mappings, making it accessible even to non-technical users.

Example Use Case:

- In the **Mapping Designer**, specify Workday as the source system and SAP SuccessFactors as the target.
- Drag fields from Workday (e.g., Employee_ID) and map them to their equivalents in SuccessFactors (e.g., PersonIdExternal).
- Apply transformations, such as combining First_Name and Last_Name into a single FullName field in SuccessFactors.
- Define filters to exclude inactive employees.
- Once the mapping is complete, Informatica reads Workday data, applies the defined transformations, and writes the output to SuccessFactors.

Informatica's vast library of prebuilt connectors and templates for HR systems, along with its visual interface, makes it invaluable for complex transformations. However, its licensing costs and resource requirements make it best suited for large enterprises.

3.4 Cloud vs. On-Premises Integration

With the rise of cloud-based HR systems, integration strategies have shifted significantly. Legacy on-premises integration, which relied on point-to-point connections, has given way to cloud integration models built for Software as a Service (SaaS) environments. Let's explore these two approaches.

Cloud Integration

Modern cloud integration connects SaaS HR systems like Workday, Salesforce, and ADP. These systems must flow data seamlessly to provide a 360-degree view of the employee lifecycle.

The biggest challenge in cloud integration is that organizations no longer control the systems they integrate. SaaS vendors control the APIs, data models, and release cycles, which can lead to breaking changes. To address this, organizations use integration platforms like **iPaaS** (Integration Platform as a Service) or API gateways.

Example of iPaaS Integration:

- Configure connectors for Workday, Salesforce, and ADP in an iPaaS platform like MuleSoft.
- Map data flows between systems using visual design tools.
- Deploy the integration to the iPaaS runtime environment, where it handles API calls, data translation, and error management.

iPaaS acts as a "shock absorber," insulating integrations from SaaS changes. For example, if Workday updates its API, you adjust it within the iPaaS without modifying the downstream systems.

API Gateways:

API gateways offer a single entry point for API requests, routing them to backend systems while managing security, throttling, and versioning. In an HR context, an API gateway could expose a unified "Employee API" that consolidates data from Workday, Salesforce, and ADP. This simplifies integration while enabling consistent security and governance policies.

On-Premises Integration

On-premises integration connects systems hosted within the corporate network, such as legacy HR systems or custom-built applications.

Advantages:

- Full control over infrastructure, governance, and security.
- Flexibility to create custom integrations tailored to unique business processes.

Challenges:

- High costs for infrastructure, software, and skilled personnel.
- Complex, time-consuming development cycles.
- Difficulty in integrating older systems with siloed data and incompatible formats.

Despite its limitations, on-premises integration remains relevant for organizations with strict data control requirements.

Chapter 4: Best Practices and Implementation Guide

4.1 An Integration Roadmap

A well-structured roadmap is the cornerstone of successful HRIS integration. It serves as the foundation for all subsequent implementation activities and helps organizations avoid common pitfalls that can derail integration projects. When developing an integration roadmap for systems like Workday, SAP SuccessFactors, or Oracle HR, organizations must balance their current needs with future requirements.

An integration roadmap typically spans three phases: discovery, optimization, and implementation. During the discovery phase, organizations must gain a comprehensive understanding of their HRIS system landscape, including all data sources, systems, and processes that need integration. For example, a multinational corporation using SAP SuccessFactors may need to map integrations with local payroll systems, time and attendance platforms, and future learning management systems.

This roadmap must include specific deliverables and milestones. For instance, a mid-sized company transitioning to Workday might plan for core HR data integration in the first quarter, payroll integration in the second, and talent management integration in the third. A phased approach reduces complexity and ensures stable deployment.

Key Components of an Effective Integration Roadmap:

- **Timeline and Dependencies**: Establish realistic timelines for project phases, ensuring interdependent tasks are properly sequenced. For example, integrating employee master data should precede payroll integration.
- **Resource Allocation**: Clearly define roles and responsibilities for technical and business stakeholders, including integration specialists, data analysts, and subject matter experts.
- **Success Metrics**: Set measurable success criteria, such as data accuracy rates, system response times, and automation levels.
- **Risk Mitigation Strategies**: Identify potential risks and develop fallback plans. For instance, if payroll integration fails, contingency plans should ensure minimal disruption.

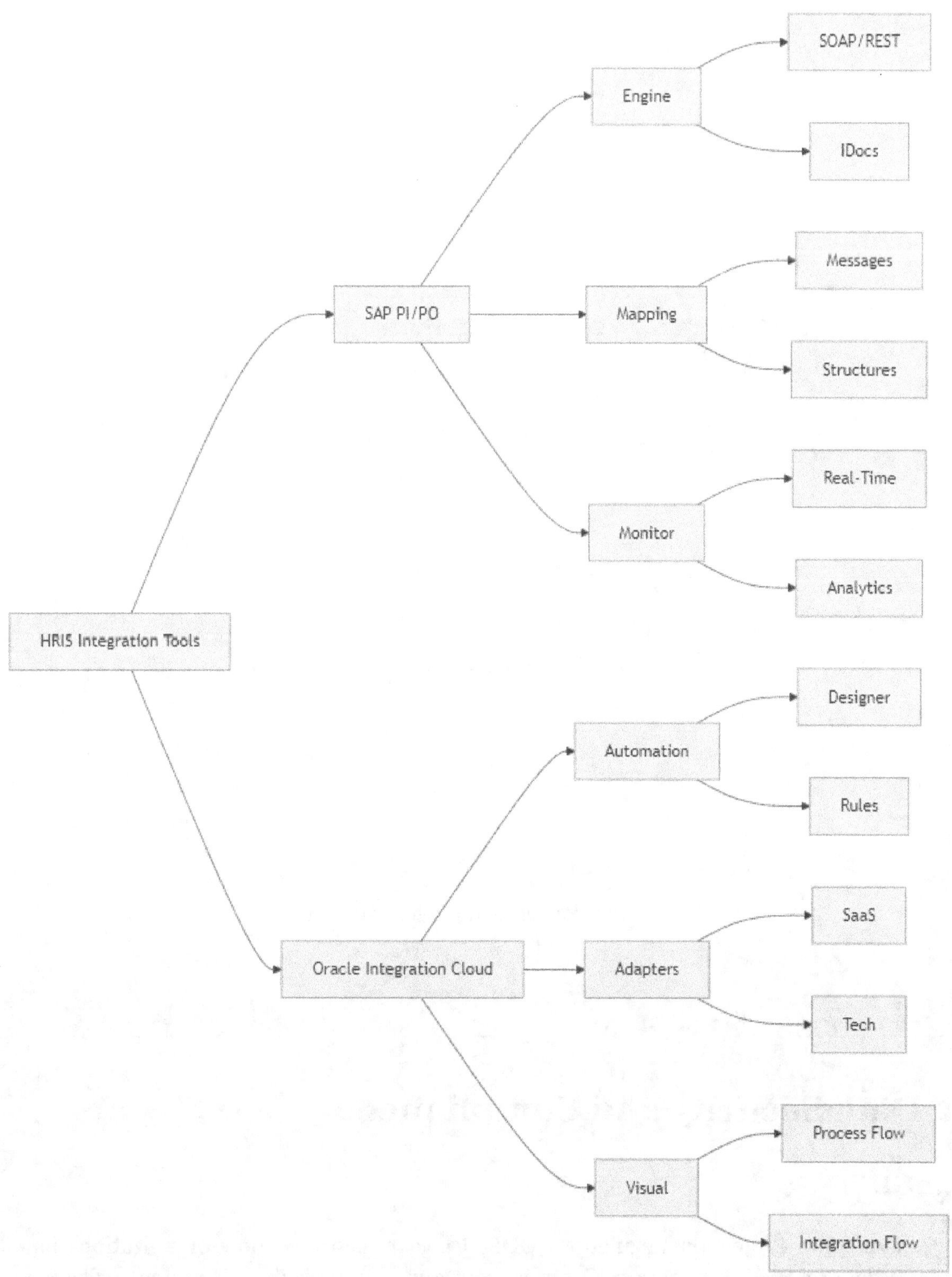

Fig: HRIS Integration Tools Overview - SAP PI/PO and Oracle Integration Cloud

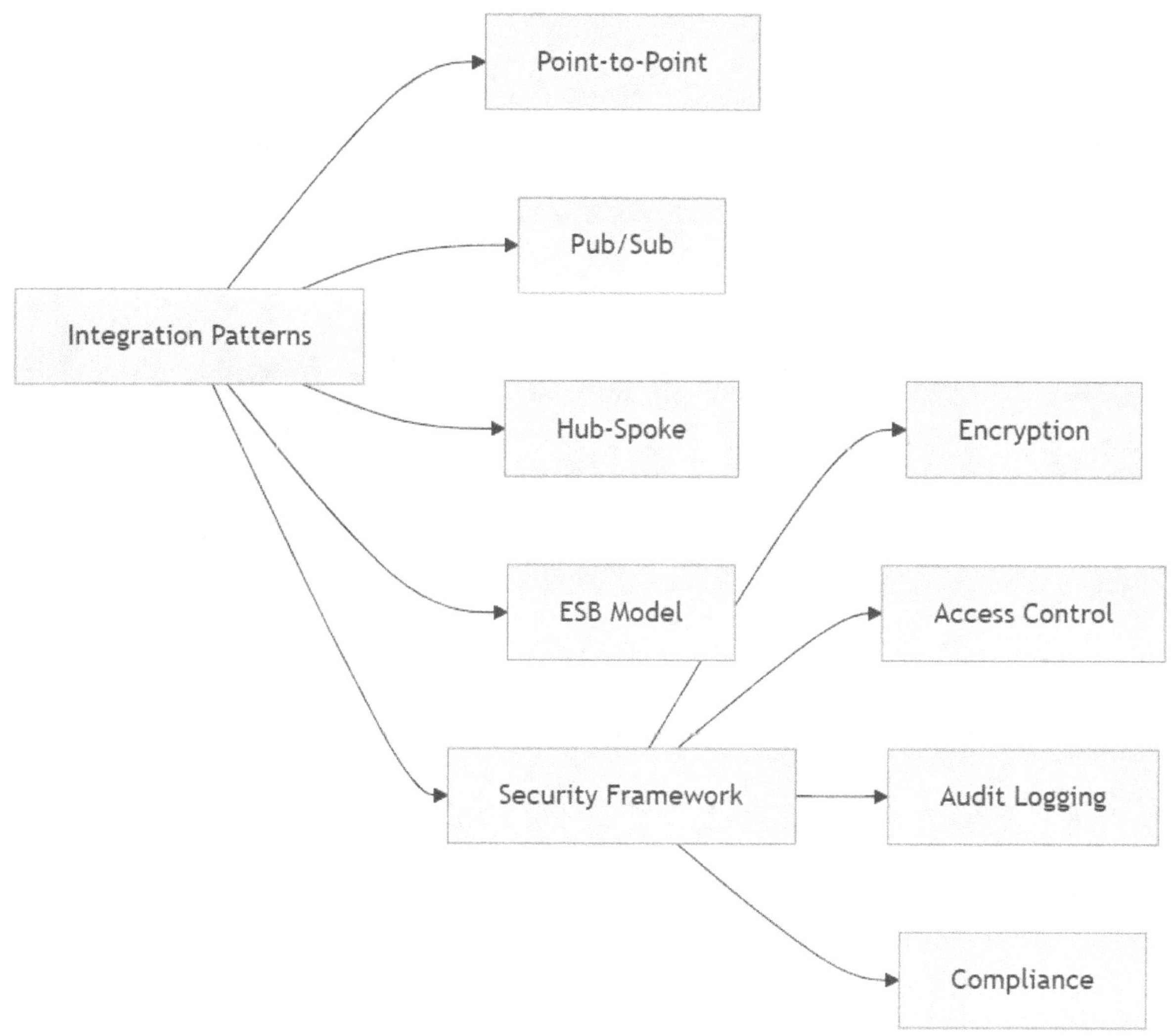

Fig: Integration Patterns and Security Framework

4.2 Data Security and Compliance

4.2.1 GDPR

The General Data Protection Regulation (GDPR) has transformed how organizations handle employee data in HRIS integration. Compliance requires organizations to adopt principles of "data protection by design and default" when integrating systems like SAP SuccessFactors or Oracle HR.

Key Considerations for GDPR-Compliant HRIS Integrations:

- **Data Minimization**: Integration workflows should transfer only the necessary personal data. For example, when integrating Workday with a learning management system, only relevant details like employee ID and job role should be shared.
- **Data Retention**: Enforce data retention policies by automating archival or deletion of historical data, such as removing old records from SAP SuccessFactors after a predefined retention period.
- **Consent Management**: Implement processes to track and manage employee consent, especially for cross-border data transfers.
- **Right to Be Forgotten**: Design integration frameworks to handle data deletion requests efficiently. For instance, if an employee requests data deletion, the framework should ensure their information is removed from all connected platforms.

4.2.2 SOC 2

SOC 2 compliance is essential for organizations handling sensitive employee data. Integration solutions should adhere to SOC 2's five trust principles: security, availability, processing integrity, confidentiality, and privacy.

Implementation Considerations for SOC 2-Compliant Integrations:

- **Access Controls**: Use role-based access control (RBAC) to enforce the principle of least privilege. For example, Workday integration service accounts should have limited permissions.
- **Audit Trails**: Maintain comprehensive logs of all data transfers and transformations, particularly when integrating sensitive systems like HRIS and payroll.
- **Encryption Standards**: Apply industry-standard encryption for data in transit and at rest. For example, when Oracle HR integrates with third-party benefits providers, data should be encrypted using protocols like TLS 1.3.

4.3 Bridging the Gap Between HR and IT

Successful HRIS integration projects require strong collaboration between HR and IT teams. While HR focuses on business processes and employee experience, IT manages technical infrastructure and system architecture. To bridge these differing perspectives:

- **Create a Joint Governance Structure**: Form a steering committee comprising HR leaders, IT architects, and business analysts. For example, when implementing SAP SuccessFactors, involve both HR process owners and IT stakeholders in decision-making.
- **Develop Shared KPIs**: Define metrics meaningful to both departments, such as process automation rates for HR and system uptime for IT.
- **Establish Regular Communication Channels**: Schedule structured meetings (e.g., biweekly status updates) and use shared project dashboards to ensure alignment. Tailor technical discussions to reflect business impact and vice versa.

4.4 Maintaining Integration

Strong monitoring and maintenance are critical for ensuring the long-term success of HRIS integrations. Proactive monitoring mechanisms can identify and resolve issues before they disrupt business operations.

Key Aspects of Integration Monitoring and Maintenance:

- **Performance Monitoring**: Track integration metrics such as API latency and success rates, especially when working with multiple downstream systems.
- **Error Handling and Resolution**: Configure automated alerts for integration failures, establish escape routes, and maintain robust troubleshooting guides.
- **Change Management**: Develop processes to manage system updates across platforms. For example, if Oracle HR releases a new API version, plan updates to ensure compatibility with existing integrations.
- **Data Quality Monitoring**: Perform regular data quality checks to ensure consistency across systems. Automated reconciliation reports comparing employee data between HRIS and payroll systems can be invaluable.
- **Documentation and Knowledge Management**: Maintain detailed records of integration architectures, configurations, and troubleshooting procedures for long-term maintenance.
- **Future-Proofing**: Design system architectures to accommodate future technological advancements. For example, consider how APIs or microservices could enhance emerging integration patterns.

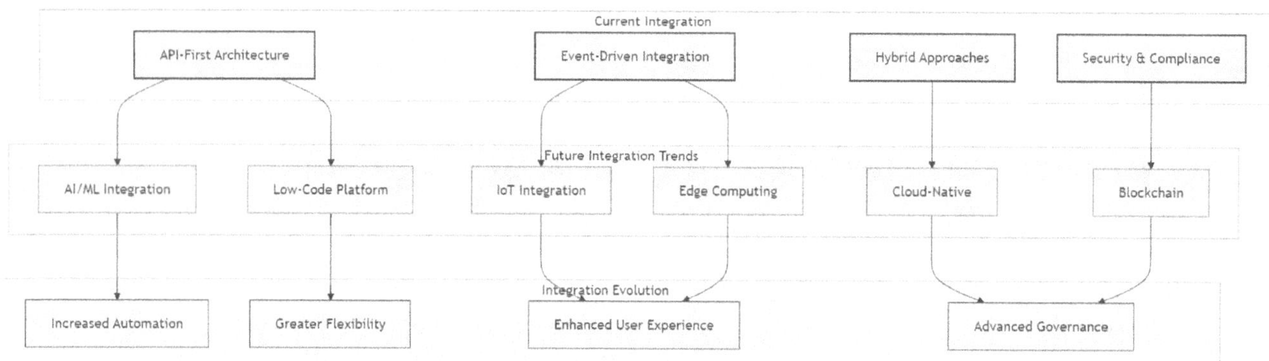

Fig: Future Integration Trends

Conclusion

1. Recap of Key Integration Patterns

This book has guided you through the intricate world of HRIS integration patterns, exploring both architectural and implementation strategies. From simple point-to-point connections to complex enterprise-wide architectures, we've seen an evolution of integration patterns that address various business needs.

Core Integration Patterns

1. **API-First Architecture**
   With the rise of API-first architecture, HRIS systems like Workday and SAP SuccessFactors are now integral to enterprise ecosystems. REST APIs have become the backbone of real-time integrations, enabling:
   - Seamless employee data synchronization.
   - Real-time payroll processing.
   - Instant updates to benefit enrollment.
   - Dynamic organizational management.
2. **Event-Driven Integration**
   Event-driven architectures provide efficient data propagation and process automation. Key use cases include:
   - Employee lifecycle event processing.
   - Automated workflow triggers.
   - Real-time compliance monitoring.
3. **Hybrid Integration**
   Organizations are increasingly combining integration patterns to address diverse business needs:
   - Real-time APIs for critical updates.
   - Batch processing for large-scale data movement.
   - Event-driven workflows for automation.
   - ESB-based routing for complex transformations.

Security and Compliance Achievements

The patterns discussed have demonstrated robust capabilities for ensuring security and compliance, including:

- GDPR-compliant data handling.
- SOC 2 controls implementation.
- Secure data transmission protocols.
- Comprehensive audit trails.

2. Future Trends in HRIS Integration

As HRIS integration continues to evolve, several trends and emerging technologies will shape its future.

Evolution of API Connectivity

The future of API-led connectivity in HRIS integration will include:

- Increased use of GraphQL for efficient data queries.
- Microservices architecture for HR systems.
- Expansion of HR API marketplaces.
- Adoption of advanced API security standards.

Artificial Intelligence and Machine Learning

AI and ML will transform HRIS integration by:

- Automating data mapping and transformation.
- Detecting and correcting errors intelligently.
- Enabling predictive maintenance for integrations.
- Optimizing workflows dynamically.

Low-Code/No-Code Integration

The democratization of integration development will continue through:

- Visual integration builders with drag-and-drop design.
- Empowering "citizen integrators" to create solutions.
- Lowering the technical barrier for HR teams.

Cloud-Native Integration Patterns

Future integrations will leverage cloud-native capabilities, including:

- Serverless architectures.
- Container-based integration services.
- Dynamic scaling and cloud-native security controls.

Emerging Technologies Impact

1. **Blockchain**
   - Secure credential verification.
   - Smart contracts for HR processes.
   - Decentralized identity management.
2. **Internet of Things (IoT)**

- o Work presence detection and attendance automation.
- o Integration with physical security systems.

3. **5G and Edge Computing**
    - o Real-time mobile HR applications.
    - o Edge-based data processing for better latency.

Evolution of Integration Governance

Governance models will emphasize:

- DevOps for HR integrations.
- Automated compliance monitoring.
- Real-time analytics and self-healing integration patterns.

Looking Ahead

The future of HRIS integration will be characterized by:

1. **Increased Automation**
    - o Self-operating integrations requiring no manual intervention.
    - o AI-driven predictive maintenance and optimization.
2. **Enhanced Security**
    - o Zero-trust architecture.
    - o Blockchain verification.
    - o Advanced encryption and automated compliance.
3. **Improved User Experience**
    - o Seamless cross-system interactions.
    - o Real-time data availability.
    - o Unified and mobile-first employee experiences.
4. **Greater Flexibility**
    - o Adaptable integration patterns.
    - o Multi-cloud support.
    - o Plug-and-play integration components.

This book provides a foundation for organizations to think strategically about their integration needs and future trends. By choosing the right patterns for specific business requirements and remaining flexible to adopt emerging technologies, HRIS integration can drive both operational efficiency and employee satisfaction.

As HR systems evolve, so will the patterns described in this book. Organizations that leverage these patterns will ensure their HR systems remain secure, scalable, and effective, supporting their business goals and employees in an ever-changing digital workplace.

Appendix A: Real World Integration Patterns

This diagram illustrates comprehensive enterprise integration patterns for Workday and SAP SuccessFactors with various downstream and upstream systems. The patterns show real-world data flows, integration methods, and system interactions commonly found in large enterprises. The architecture demonstrates both cloud-to-cloud and cloud-to-on-premise integration scenarios, along with various integration methods including real-time APIs, event-driven patterns, and batch processes.

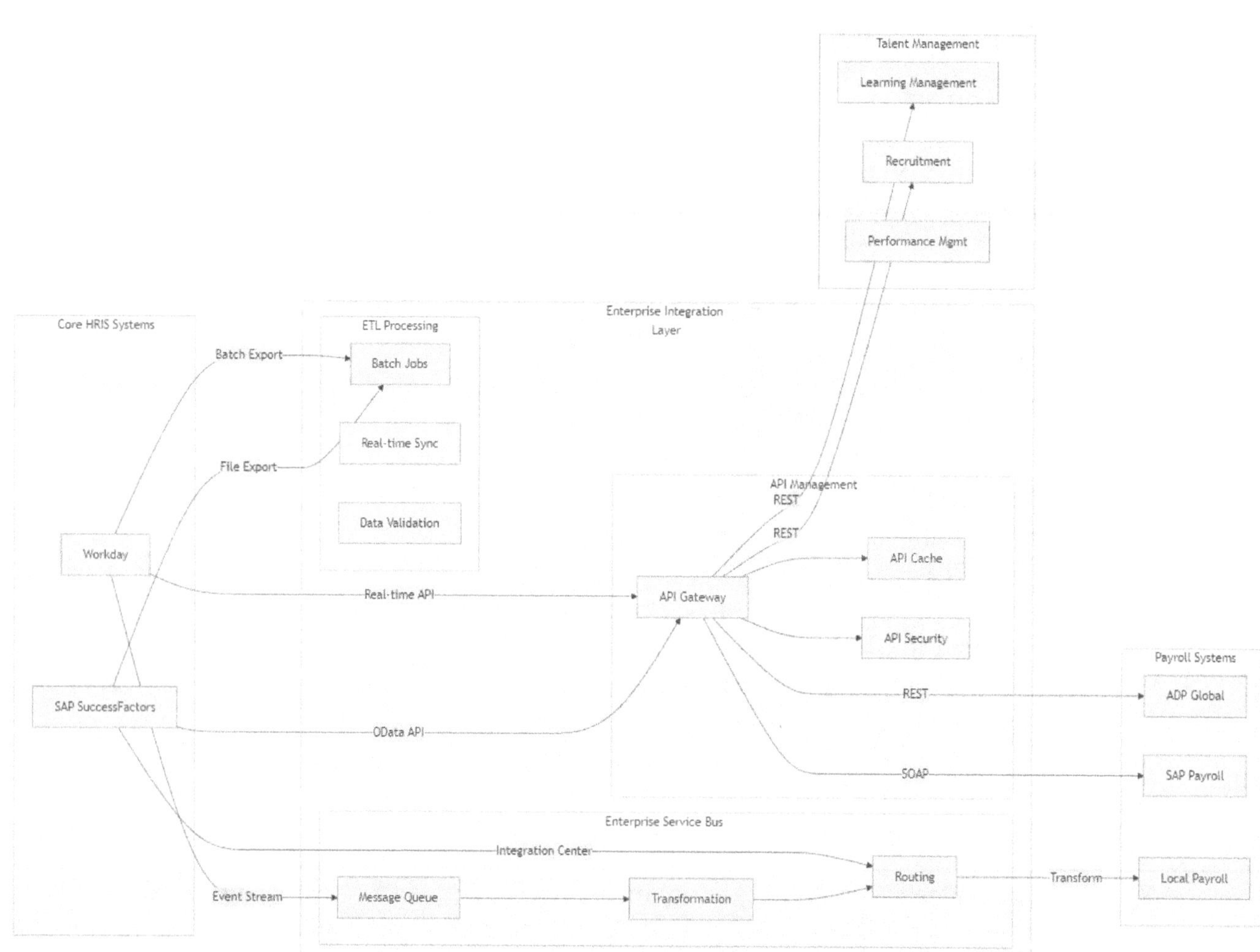

Diagram 1: Core HRIS Systems and Integration Layer

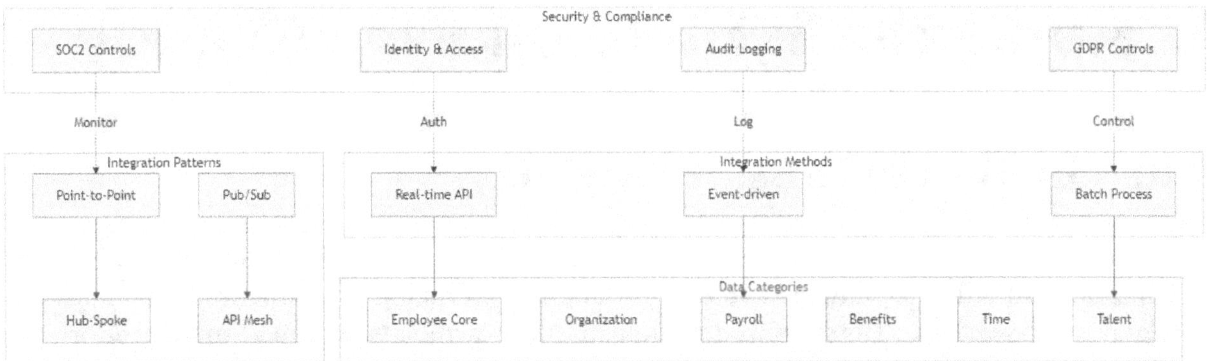

Diagram 2: Security, Compliance, and Supporting Integration Concepts

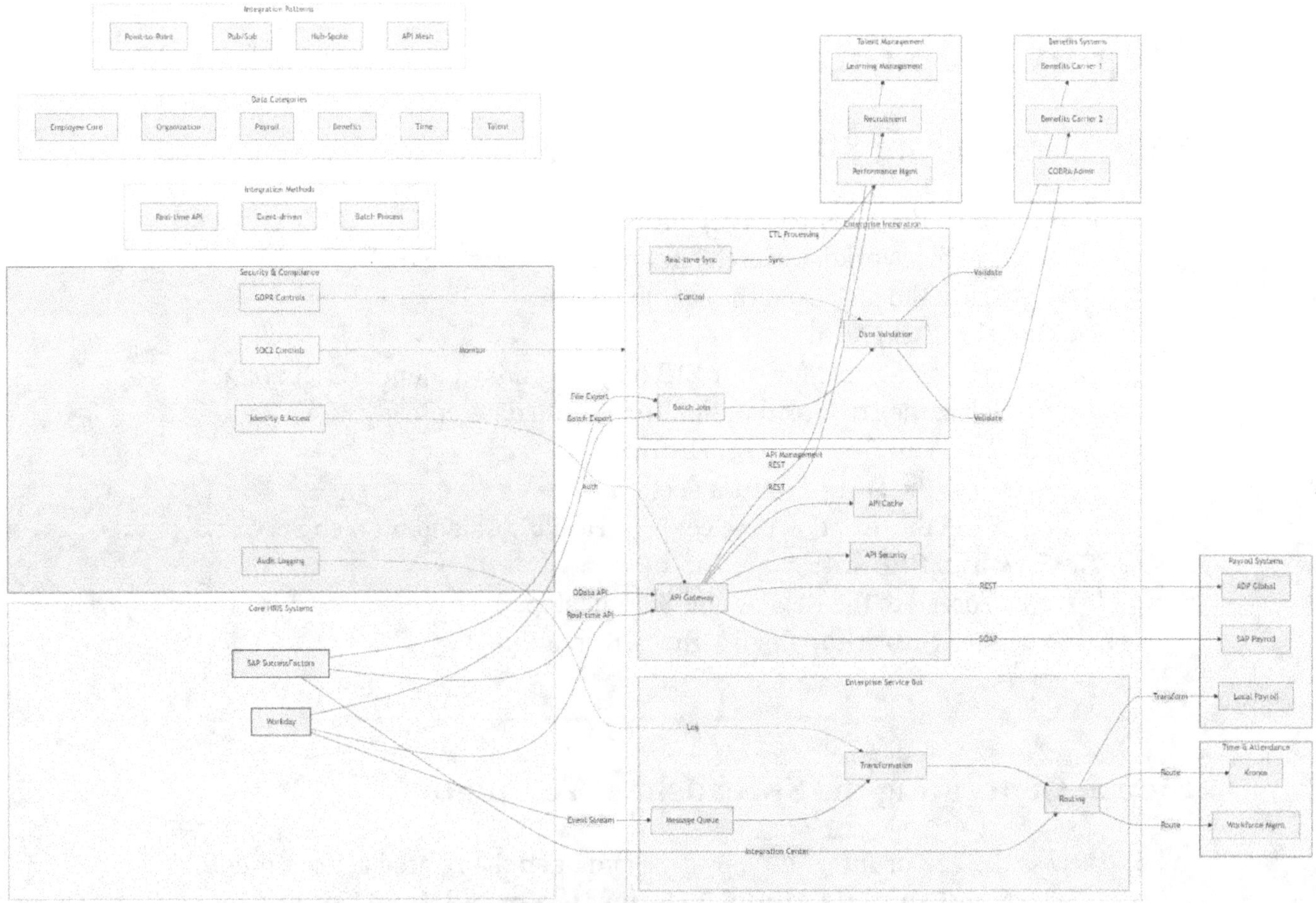

Diagram 3: HRIS Integration Patterns

Appendix B: EIB Tutorial in Workday

Introduction to EIBs in Workday

The Enterprise Interface Builder (EIB) is a powerful tool within Workday that allows organizations to efficiently import and export data. By leveraging preconfigured templates and Workday's web services, EIBs simplify data uploads and downloads, minimize manual effort, and reduce errors.

This tutorial walks you through the steps required to create and update holiday calendars using EIB. It covers creating an EIB, generating a spreadsheet template, populating it with data, and uploading the changes into Workday.

Step-by-Step Guide

Step 1: Creating an EIB

1. **Navigate to the Create EIB Task**:
    - Use the Workday search bar and type "Create EIB."
    - Select the task from the search results.
2. **Define the EIB Details**:
    - Provide a name for your EIB (e.g., "Holiday Calendar EIB 2023").
    - Select the **Inbound** option to indicate data upload.
3. **Select the Web Service Operation**:
    - Go to the **Data Format** section.
    - From the dropdown, select "Put Holiday Calendar (Web Service)."
4. **Review and Submit**:
    - Proceed to the Review and Submit step.
    - Click **Submit** to finalize the EIB creation.

Step 2: Generating the Spreadsheet Template

1. Access the EIB or Integration System and open the related actions menu.
2. Navigate to **Template Model** > **Generate Spreadsheet Template**.
3. Confirm the operation and click **OK**.
4. A notification will appear in the top-right corner when the template is ready.
5. Download the spreadsheet template from the provided link.

Step 3: Populating the Spreadsheet

1. Open the downloaded spreadsheet template.
2. Populate the spreadsheet with the required details for each holiday, including:
   - **Holiday Name**: For example, "New Year's Day."
   - **Date**: Enter the exact date of the holiday.
   - **Country or Region**: Assign the calendar to a specific country or region.
3. Save the completed spreadsheet in .xlsx format.

Step 4: Uploading the Spreadsheet

1. Return to the **Integration System** page.
2. Open the related actions menu and navigate to **Integration** > **Launch/Schedule**.
3. In the **Integration Attachments** section, click **Create Integration Attachment**.
4. Upload the populated spreadsheet and click **OK**.

Step 5: Monitoring and Verifying the EIB Execution

1. Refresh the Integration System page to check the EIB execution status.
2. If errors occur, download the error report for detailed troubleshooting.
3. Once successful, verify the updated holidays in the **View Holiday Calendar** task.

Best Practices for EIBs

- **Validate Data**: Always ensure the spreadsheet data is correct before uploading.
- **Standardize Templates**: Use consistent naming conventions and date formats across all templates.
- **Leverage Error Reports**: If issues arise, use error reports to quickly identify and resolve problems.

Visual Representation of the Process

1. **Create EIB**: Define the integration parameters in Workday.
2. **Generate Template**: Download the preformatted spreadsheet.
3. **Populate Data**: Enter the necessary details into the spreadsheet.
4. **Upload Data**: Use EIB to upload the data into Workday.
5. **Verify Results**: Check the holiday calendar updates for accuracy.

Conclusion

This tutorial simplifies the process of using Workday EIBs for holiday calendar updates, empowering HR teams to save time and enhance data accuracy. By following this structured approach, organizations can ensure seamless execution and minimal errors. For more advanced use cases, such as recurring uploads or integrations with third-party systems, consider exploring Workday Studio or API-based solutions.

Author Bio

Sudheer Devaraju is a seasoned HR Information Systems architect with over 11 years of experience in designing and implementing HR integrations for global organizations including Fortune 1 companies. With certifications in Workday, SAP, and advanced API integration, Sudheer has a deep understanding of what it takes to build scalable, efficient HR ecosystems.

Beyond consulting, Sudheer is deeply committed to sharing his expertise through various channels. He contributes to the field by authoring books, publishing research papers, providing peer review feedback to industry experts, mentoring colleagues at Walmart, and conducting workshops.